also by Roger Roloff

Gathered from the Wild:
Poems of a Wanderer

The Poetry of Earth

Natural Gifts

Illuminations

Earthcraft

Heartwood: New and Selected Poems

Natural Voice (compact disc)

For Don and Carol,
dedicated readers —
Roger
Apr. 7, 2019

Windflowers

Happy trails from Roger Roloff

Roger Roloff

Illustrations by Rachel Hunderfund

2018

SHIRES✷PRESS

ShiresPress
4869 Main Street
P.O. Box 2200
Manchester Center, VT 05255

PUBLISHER'S NOTE: *Windflowers* is a work of fiction. Names, characters, places, and incidents are either the product of the author's imagination or are used fictitiously, and any resemblance to actual persons (living or dead), events, or locales is entirely coincidental.

ISBN 978-1-60571-432-5

To the Master-Mistress of Our Garden
—for B.A.P.—

No human mother-soul can take her place
as shaper of this gift of good homeland.
See where lamb's ears and bee balm grant air space
hummingbirds claim—though bees are hardly banned.
Forsythia hosts catbird songs and nests
near always open arms of arbor vitae:
shelter in summer for robin redbreasts,
in winter for snowbirds when winds are mighty.

Cleared patches of our ground put me to work
on rows of greens and other tender crops;
she teaches and I learn, like Chaucer's Clerk,
and this fair trade we practice never stops.

No one should cross her aims and strong, wise hands;
for these gifts my manhood has stood, and stands.

Contents

Foreword

By early May along the Vernooy Kill in New York's Ulster County, colonies of windflowers are usually in bloom, standing perhaps six inches above leaf litter. On a sunny day the scattered patches of white blossoms provide a starry accompaniment— silent but radiant—to the sparkling Kill's constant *mezzo forte* of rushing water.

A closer look at a few of these small perennial flowers— typically with five petal-like sepals suggesting stars—reveals that they have notable differences: shorter or longer stems; leaves sometimes divided into three or five sharply toothed segments (the latter matching, fittingly, the plant's Latin name of *Anemone quinquefolia*); and variously glowing centers, reflecting differing numbers of pistils and stamens. What wood anemones (another of their English names) have in common—whether their native ground adjoins trout streams like the Vernooy Kill or as-yet-leafless thickets or woods edges—is a heightened sensitivity to winds of small sizes: at times so finely attuned I'd swear there *isn't* the slightest breath of air. But windflowers can't lie; moreover, their thin stems, trembling in apparent stillness, remind me that awareness of subtler, unsensed truth— call it a poetic dimension— can and does surpass literal, surface perception, even by humans.

Despite this delicate sense of touch, windflowers remain hardy, persistent colonizers of their favored ground. If a large oak collapses on their patch, the flowers nevertheless find ways to bloom the following spring. Then again, they have heralded the season far longer than *Homo sapiens* has known it, and should continue to achieve their lovely annual rebirth for ages to come.

The arrangement of windflowers on the land—though often scattered or in small groups—sometimes resembles a dense cluster of stars, in the most striking cases as if radiating from their galactic cores. As with such botanical galaxies, so with figurative flowers on printed pages, proceeding as their roots and seeds of thought suggest: this is an old and organic way of poetic birth, growth, and procreation. And as always by virtue of the musical speech of poetry, readers have a built-in and inclusive choice: to absorb and contemplate the meanings silently, or to enliven anew these flowers of the mind with the wind of their own voices.

Windflowers

The Crossway

Only a throwback thought of doing this work:
someone who didn't care for fancy tools,
or didn't see the need to build a bridge,
or even see the sense in drawing plans.
Those would be overkill, a waste of skill.
This shallow swamp deserved a gentler touch,
provided by the wood it grew so well.
Red cedar (Juniper to botanists)
had filled the wet land time and time again,
and generations of it lay or leaned,
quite dead, on mossy acres underneath
new timber—some hardwood, but mostly cedar.
These trees he'd leave to live and die in peace,
for dead trunks, slow to rot, would meet his need.

No matter where he stood and aimed his gaze,
a straight way through the swamp from edge to edge
could not be made: one large pine stood against it,
so a curving path took shape in his mind's eye.
This spared the mighty, whispering giant's ground
(with knobby surface roots), but cost more labor
in cutting straight-cored, four-foot cedar logs.
He split these in the middle, end to end,
with iron wedges hammered through the halves.
Placing the split sides snugly down, crosswise
to footsteps, made a path called corduroy
which slowly took the contours of a snake,
its gently sinuous length of forty paces
winding through woods: here skirting frost-heaved roots,
there easing by a rock.

                    He worked all winter,
borrowing time from putting up firewood
for next year, shoveling snow, feeding the woodstove.

1

Those borrowed hours repaid him as he'd hoped
when water from snow melt and April rains
drained through the scores of scavenged cedar planks,
yet let him cross dryshod, his cart in tow.
The beauty of it was freely reusing
sound fragments on hand, waiting to be noticed,
shaped carefully, and put in the right order—
as if his work expressed the land's long thought.
"The crossway fits the landscape naturally,"
his neighbors, near and far, still sum it up—
and that, in truth, is music to his ears.

On Memory Lane

My love and I'd walk back
in time and space to place
a memory grown slack
which more years would erase.
At least this was our thought
for white wildflowers we sought.

The path there, long and winding,
passed rattlesnake rock-piles
that kept us fully minding
each step along oak aisles
by nooks of wintergreen
with new leaves, striped and lean.

Carpets of partridge-berries,
some with last autumn's fruit,
peeked from leaf duff which carries
more hidden spring, to boot,
in mosses by the yard
and shinleaves, still unscarred.

Though evergreen, these signs
of early April cheered
our hearts. But skeptic minds
asked: would that ground we neared
show lacy leaves, with flowers
hung out to dry all hours?

Or would that memory,
enlarged by distant youth
and dreams of what might be,
outlast the simple truth
of plants that lose their hold
to others, new and old?

The final stretch, downslope,
seemed one long path of brown,
and so with sinking hope
we glumly shuffled down.
Yet as the end drew near
small leaf-lace did appear,

then stalks like wee clotheslines
with tiny pantaloons:
white blossoms' odd designs
we'd found so many moons
ago when their green laces
spanned roughly twenty paces.

These flowers through which we strode
two hundred steps outnumbered
the rest by this woods road—
though later blooms still slumbered,
waiting till more light warms
their widely varied forms.

And our old memory
of where one spring we'd gone
had been (wide eyes could see)
far, far improved upon,
as wild Earth sometimes teaches—
that day with Dutchman's-breeches.

Windflowers

—for Juli Gallagher—

Somehow they rise unbidden from leaf litter
to try the sun and air of still-bare woods.
Their inching spring may well turn cold and bitter,
losing brief warmth to winter's latitudes.
But drawn by longer days and stronger rays,
they sense the season offers more than sleep
and risk the elements' capricious ways
as trembling stems and light leaves upward creep.

Their sole ambition is one small white flower,
not minding if its measured days are crisper,
and glad for any sun or April shower.
It's stirred by young spring's slightest sigh or whisper
and loyal to the roots of home rebirth,
sustaining ground of being in old Earth.

The Lane Between Stone Rows

Back when hill farmers cleared these slopes and hollows,
a double fencerow made a useful border.
The ground between two stone rows your eye follows
marks where good neighbors shared a lane in order
to lead their herds and wagons field to field.
Thin, rocky soil—best used for crops of hay
or timber—pastured stock that ate and wheeled
fresh timothy on many a summer day.
Then trees came down for charcoal, so the hills
grew grassier—though herds had little shade.
Years later, trees' seed banks proved their strong wills,
reclothing this ridge as it's now arrayed.
The stone rows didn't budge, but added moss
while keeping flowers to tell the seasons by.
Spring beauties bathe in April's sun and cross
far into fields on both sides, as I spy.
Trout lilies lead to brookside bishop's caps
in May, when tulip trees spread wide their petals,
and toothwort's deep-cleft leaves fade and collapse.
Pink lady's-slippers' bloom by mid-June settles
into a seed pod on each spent flower's stem.
By then large swaths of steeplebush are rising,
and milkweed blossoms perfume air near them.
Turtlehead mouths past mild fall are downsizing,
while gentians' closed blooms hide in many a nook.
And when a killing frost makes asters rest,
the stone-marked lane remains an open book
to read cold seasons through from east to west—
as it has been as long as these hills gave
good lives and livings to sons of the soil.
The twin rows have their uses still, and save
a flowering way to keep foot-travelers loyal.

Beyond the Trail

Why was I so surprised?
Perhaps because the road
I traveled, wagon-sized,
bent where a small brook flowed
in late day, almost still—
until it leapt downhill

into a deep ravine
I hadn't guessed at, shaded
up high by hemlocks' screen.
Nothing, I saw, invaded
steep banks but ferns, shed leaves,
sparse trees: no human thieves.

Just low November sun
explored the slopes and stream
till dusk and day seemed one.
Then came a last, long beam,
and falling water glistened.
I stayed and watched and listened.

I'm glad whoever owns
the glen keeps hands off, too,
for there are old, deep zones
a footpath would undo:
better to save this sight
and sound of fall twilight.

A Hunter's Tale

"Vaguely related to the human race,"
old Cyrus dubbed himself with a worn straight face
one winter night as we walked at his place.
"I don't pretend to be its advocate;
let's hope our planet gets a better fate."

I sighed, "How did we get to such a state?"

"Try talking with the Busybodies of . . .
Their LORD, soul savers for the Great Above,"
Cyrus sighed back. "I'll call them that to you—
those preying hands they'd lay on fast like glue—
and tell you of two dames I saw downslope
whose rising heads—each one a periscope—
revealed spry crones I'll christen Faith and Hope.
These ladies, smiling, braved my gravel drive
with their good news, unwilling 'to deprive
me of its joy,' they beamed as I, ambushed
in Swiss chard, wondered (not aloud) what pushed
their proselytizing zeal on lucky me?
'I've got my hands full here, as you can see,'
I called; 'give me a moment, if you can.'

'Nice garden,' flattered Hope.
                              'All by one man?'
Faith coyly asked.
                    'Yes, ma'am; it feeds me well,'
I countered, drawing near. 'And I must tell
you both, it's my good news these forty years
since I began full-time outdoor careers:
tending my gardens, woodlot, nearby streams
and forests—every day pursuing dreams
of thoughtful living on this gift of land.
I'm guessing that you ladies understand

how much hard work's involved: the grass-fed beef
your people raise.'
        'But now,' Faith purred, 'our chief
herd animals are sheep. They graze, in brief,
far better on steep land.'
        'Your profit's grown,
no doubt: high yield from wool to marrowbone.
How thrifty! getting all that can be taken—
to shake loose every dollar to be shaken.
And it must cost you, well, a pretty penny
to power and feed and clothe and house so many
believers, giving most of what they've earned
and saved—'
        Here Hope broke in, whose large eyes burned
with strange light: 'Yes, some give up everything
to save their places—all that they can bring.'

'As much as that,' I said, my voice grown soft.
Silence prevailed a moment.
        Then Faith coughed,
continuing, 'Which brings us back to you,
alone here on this high land with its view
of mountain ranges—'
        'If you really knew,'
I barged in, 'you would see I'm never lonely.
While scavenging dead oaks for firewood, only
I see fresh scat from foxes; or in spring
when gathering ramps, then I hear grosbeaks sing
strongly and deeply from ardent rose breasts;
and when I pull my arrows from the chests
of deer or bear, I sample wildling apples
they craved. Call me Old Adam, one who grapples
with Mother Earth on her own ancient terms

respectfully—and hopes his way affirms.
Without the partnership of this good ground
and what's on it, and under, and around,
I couldn't live. Beyond a need for people,
I cherish still a shrub whose flowering steeple
I dare not eat, but bees keep for their good.
Pain drugs I get from what's worse yet, monkshood!
Two corn snakes, slithering in my compost bin,
I thank for keeping ranks of rodents thin.
And squirrels I haven't shot and skinned for stew
plant white oak acorns, and I'm glad they do.
In short, I try hard to respect wild boarders:
to balance, gently, wild and man-made orders.'

'But don't those grand peaks steer your thinking higher?'
Faith pressed on doggedly.
                 'I'd be a liar
if I put down the sun and sky, of course,'
I shot back, 'Source and shield of our life-force,
but they're not what you're driving at, I'm sure.
Your godly vision lacks a living lure
to place my faith in heaven so abstract.
I'll take the one this world has always backed,
not perfect but kept going by five senses.
A wiser man than I shunned high pretenses:
Religion's how a man spends his free time,
he claimed, and I'll add, doing that's no crime.'

Hope looked at Faith rather dejectedly,
and I said, 'Let's agree to disagree
without hard feelings. I have garden chores,
if you'll excuse me. Yet—the vast outdoors
awaits us all. Stay here awhile and watch
Twin Mountain; eagles may fly through its notch.'

So there's my tale from start to not-quite-end,
for as we know, my flower-loving friend,
old Earth is too beholden to the play
man can't outgrow called predator and prey.
I didn't have the heart, at the last minute,
to tell those poor sheep how they're caught up in it."

Cy shook his head beneath the star-filled sky,
then pointed to Orion, standing high.

Twilight Clarity

—for Robert Fearneyhough—

Dreaming I'd spy a cloudless sky
I woke before one winter dawn
and, rubbing sand from each tired eye,
I saw clear evening's promise kept:
some western stars were bright, not wan.
Fast warmly clad and shod I stepped
into the twilight, cold and still.
Southeast but low its prizes hovered,
unseen as yet, and so uphill
a quarter-mile my quick steps covered.
The eastern glow I strode toward
touched sleeping houses all the way.
No mystery here: my neighbors snored
and slept, since it was no workday
but one of rest. My early waking,
however, neared its own reward:
not dawn but crescent moonlight breaking
through pines, that bare boughs sliced and scored.
The moon itself was in the clear
a few steps on, its southward curve
pointing to Venus, shining near—
two fingers' width right, as they serve
at arm's length, held at shoulder height.
Thus taking in the heavenly pair
I sought one more celestial light,
discreet and fleet, I knew was there.
Yet when I stooped or leaned or stood
on tiptoes, some thick-crowned hardwood
still forced me to lay just mind's-eyes on
what gleamed behind the treed horizon.
So I missed seeing Mercury,
but well-trained eyes more highly placed,
I knew, had marveled at all three
dead, shining spheres so closely spaced.

The firm Earth I stood on, though, far
more rare than any lifeless star
as well, maintained a view of trees
unknown on doomed infinities.
And the glow before this Earthly dawn
backlighting woods with hints of pink
hushed slow footsteps from where I'd gone
for worlds that made me stop and think
most of the one I'm living on.

The Western Lights

Adeline: Still got your head in that newspaper, Rafe?
Come over here and have a look at this.

Rafe: Don't be impatient, Adeline; we might
just see *aurora borealis* soon,
it says here. Sunspots are quite active now.

A.: Unless they're flaring in the next two minutes,
you're going to miss a gorgeous spectacle,
and it won't cost you one red cent, besides.

R.: Neither will Northern Lights, if I wake up—

A.: How often have you done that, honestly?
What I remember is you, sleeping on—

R.: Nonsense! there was that time in eighty-nine,
when all night long we watched sky curtains dancing—

A.: But you were up already, like the neighbors;
nobody had to set alarm clocks then.
Now, come on, dear, get off your duff and see
this sunset painting almost everything!

(A pregnant pause—till Rafe arrives and looks.)

R.: My goodness, Addie, now I understand:
the heavens are on fire from top to bottom!
Why didn't you say so?

A.:   I did, with all
but elbows in your ribs, you stubborn man!
Look at the shades of red above the ridge;

the tower's a candle, wick and tallow glowing
at the same time—

R.:   Not with its green night light,
either; I've never seen it lit like this.

A.: The Crag, too, burns in . . . Rafe, is that vermilion?

R.: I think so, and it's coloring oak crowns,
the golden boughs of best November light.

A.: And there's our own west oak, its high crown flaming
with reds and golds, the fire grate of the sun.
How can a person not feel humble, dear,
before such power—though air pollution's partly
the reason?

R.:   Yes, I knew you'd think of that,
Addie, you scamp. Let me add my two cents:
how can a human being think he's greater
than all else out there, now illuminated?
How? Gratitude alone is what I feel:
lit up, too, witnessing what holds our lives
and livings—

A.:   Spoken like a forager
and gardener bred in the bone, of course.
Wise use is all you want from this good land,
not ownership that squanders fertile soil.
And by the way, do you think *this* sunset
might top the Northern Lights for colors, Rafe?

R.: No doubt about it, and it's cheaper, sure,
than paying for a trip to Nome or Fairbanks.

A.: I told you so: we've seen the *Western Lights*—
together—for the price of dwelling here.
That's not a bad fringe benefit, I'd say.

R.: Which we might get once more tomorrow, eh?

Good Hours Kept in Mind

—for Carla Knudsen and Anne Ross—

Only a snapshot's left
to show a foreground full
of irises to pull
in city folks bereft
of flowers grown at home.
The white-haired man and wife
who worked these blossoms' loam
stand, as they had in life,
behind blooms and good seed
to fill that human need.
The farm this couple kept
for crops of flowers and food
till they forever slept
was hardly idle trade—
though even in smiles it paid.
Its stand where Anna stood
with Ivar's flowers is gone,
their field replanted—all
in houses on a lawn
too perfect, spring through fall.
Yet their name—Everson—
stays on a sign to blaze
where more souls than just one,
perhaps, recall bouquets
which filled the old pair's days.
And that street sign reminds
me of what can be done
along old-fashioned lines
still, in good working hours,
by cultivating flowers.

Unexpected Pay Dirt

—for B.A.P.—

She only meant to thin thug daffodils,
too thickly settled in raspberries' ground.
But with her hand tools there, how one job spills
into another! Soon her sharp eyes found
mugwort encroaching on the lower side,
so spadefuls flew beyond the fence where red
young leaves of poison ivy failed to hide.
As her long-handled weeder stopped their spread,

a many-chambered brownish fungus caught
her sweeping glance and earned a startled "Oh!"
For there, among raspberry canes, unsought
but prized, a large morel had chanced to grow.
She found five more big beauties that May Day,
and mushroom season was well underway.

Notes from the Postmaster General

Unless wild critters scorn your garden's crops,
you're going to need good fences for those neighbors.
Cute Bambi-eyes and cartoon bunny-hops
will fool you out of fruits of your hard labors
if you're not careful. That's where posts come in,
and someone setting them with a post-hole digger
to make the fence much higher than Bambi's chin—
too high to jump, as well, when he's grown bigger.
And let's face it: two stones for every dirt
describes our soil, so dig your posts in deep,
don't pound them inches—till your gloved hands hurt.
My fences, which no local deer can leap,
stand six feet high, with posts set two feet down.
No need to buy posts, either, if your woods
have rot-resistant cedar; even in town
you'd hardly ever purchase better goods.
Just cut the fallen timber, not live trees,
to proper post length, saving that expense.
Use what's on hand, I say; and if this frees
you from a middleman, you've kept good sense.
Yet digging post-holes in less fertile ground
means rock removal is your major task;
and since few neighbors have rock bars around,
you'll need to buy one, hang the price (don't ask).
Maybe you'll find one, second-hand and cheap—
as I did—holding down that hand tool's cost.
In any case, each hole you dig will reap
its share of stones, but don't let them get lost
or tossed: small ones fill in a gravel drive;
large ones build flower borders or cap walls;
and others, mid-sized—though frost heaves contrive
to tilt your posts—will prop them for long hauls
of years or decades through cold stress and strain.
So, in the end, rocks you dug out will hold

your posts upright and help your fence remain
a silent partner till your garden's old—
so old it may be tended by your heirs.
A well-built fence, whatever town folks say,
will make wild neighbors mind their own affairs
and guard your crops—from seed through harvest day.

Reading Rocks

—for Lynn Fearneyhough—

Some human quirk there is that loves a cairn.
I don't say every person does, or should—
only that people build them, not wild critters
which make their mounds on land organically.
Of course you can't help seeing either kind
of markings on a walk through woods or fields:
you're trying not to step or stumble on
them—that's more typical, I'm bound to say.
So wanderers on foot must pay attention;
at least we all might well agree on this.
But why those heaps are there is where we don't.
I'm not referring to the piles bears drop
in berry patches, marking wilder borders,
or coyote droppings placed on rocks (same thing),
but scattered groups of stones inviting thought.
Some mark a trail—it's easy to conclude—
where land grows too few trees, or none, but spreads
a bumper crop of rocks at our disposal.
Sometimes these seem disposed to baffle us:
when lines of cairns apparently converge
yet soon veer separate ways, stopping our feet.
While searching for the true path to go on,
we might see toppled cairns and not go there,
or top rocks blazed with red, and follow those,
or even borrow stones from some spilled pile—
cairn-wreckers' work is one more thing, to boot—
to make the way we guess is right guide better.
(Sometimes we guess well, sometimes not, alas.)
Then there are grander heaps built with such care
they ought to have a plaque but rarely do.
To find out who made them and why, I went
some years back to an expert's presentation.
It turned out he was mainly self-taught, though:
without a doctorate in old earth-science,

as well-schooled experts call it nowadays.
However much that counts, I watched and heard
him with all due respect for two full hours.

At first he startled me by saying "Karen"
repeatedly, but when he showed a slide,
I knew he meant what rhymes with Scottish "bairn."
More slides revealed the varied shapes and sizes
of stone piles marking borders, roads, gravesites,
memorials, and (most of all) groundwater.
He was a practiced dowser—he informed
the gathering of maybe twenty people—
so finding hidden springs and flows deep down
had long intrigued him and become his passion.
He worked stone features in here, as they marked
the lines of ancient rivers underground
not just with cairns but large rocks set at angles—
which couldn't be coincidence, he claimed.
He paced the room when telling of flow lines
he found on tribal land in Arizona;
then back and forth from us to slides he spun,
gray pony-tail flung out with each quick turn.
His high voice rose as he flashed focused flows
(the formal term he stuck to afterward)
he'd sketched on maps of Chile and Peru—
almost chanting like a revival preacher.
He fairly danced around the room like one,
inspired by all those focused flows, unseen
of course, that his long study had unearthed.
At times a bysitter would have an arm
or hand or shoulder grabbed to emphasize
the pull of those great rivers in the ground.
And so the minutes flowed by, soon half-hours
that swelled to hours before at last he funneled
his flood of words into a placid pool
for questions from the audience, subdued:
yes, not one person stirred or stood to leave.

In fact he blocked the door, shut tight as well,
as brief, respectful queries got smooth answers.
I thought he bristled somewhat, though, when asked
if other scientists had cross-examined
his findings—in the spirit of good science.
Forcing a smile, he said the rocks don't lie—
about what, he left everyone to wonder.
It seemed, in short, that skeptics were not welcome.
Then came a friendly question, and he strode—
chuckling, with head thrown back—into the group.
So finally I made the swift escape
I needed for a certain focused flow.

An Ecosystem

—in memory of Henry W. Longfellow—

Out of the bosom of old shale,
out of deep folds of layers taken,
up through thick rock-waves without fail,
oozed from their dark gray banks unshaken,
perennial springs arise and flow,
fresh waters of wetlands I know.

Five nameless swamps to nourish plants,
to catch and filter snow and rain,
to echo with spring peepers' chants
and, watering beast and man, remain
the liquid force this good land keeps
in gurgling brooks and silent seeps:

not just for what eggs and seeds store,
or for green, rooted growth alone;
not for winged, scaled, or furred lives more
than for humans to call their own
exists this remnant paradise,
wall-watered earth beyond a price.

The Human Interlude

Fourscore and seven years ago no house
sat where I write these lines in comfort now.
When it came, clearing all but a shalebank brow
it squats on, every earthworm, wren, and mouse—
if not killed outright—fled to wilder ground.
Assaulted daily by the noise and smell
of men and deadly tools—a man-made hell—
these natives watched and waited, wild lives bound.
But since their borrowed land was occupied,
the refugees made do as best they could:
at least they dwelled near their old neighborhood.
And some small creatures wandered back, unspied,
finding a crack or gap the timber frame—
though new not perfect—offered: living space
for ants or spiders. Soon mice probed the place,
wriggling inside to capture new-found game.
Mouse-hunters in their turn arrived by night,
unnoticed but for traces left behind:
owl pellets which no human eye might find,
fox urine dogs know but most folks, not quite.
Meanwhile house wrens and phoebes made their nests
in nooks and crannies any house provides;
and trees or bushes growing near all sides
trembled in spring with songs of more winged guests.
Not least the shalebank's rocky soil, scraped thin
but laced with seeds, released their growth in grasses,
as well as sprouting elms and oaks and masses
of dandelions, plantains, and their kin.
The land has stood the human interlude,
in short, which spurred craft hitherto untapped
in many clever beings to adapt.
Does this change human owners' attitude?

Gardeners who need this land to live learn best:
taking its measure, making it theirs, too
as, day by day, hand labor to renew
its life sustains their living and old quest.
One day the human interlude will end
and the globe reclaim for good a wilder state.
Far better that the day's not soon but late,
and mankind leave Earth as an old, dear friend.

People Watcher

(translated from the original tongue)

I really thought the whole crowd hopeless, too.
They act like gods and think they own the world—
drilling, digging, killing willy-nilly.
I don't blame you for calling them a plague.
We're stuck with them, and who knows when they'll leave?
I say we make the best of a bad deal
and take the crumbs we find—and maybe more.
There's this old couple, see. They don't have kids,
they don't keep pets. You know the folks I mean:
both echoing the "teakettle" song I sing.
They only feed birds suet in the winter;
their gardens, berry patches, and fruit trees
do that in summer—not so much for us,
but for the bugs and spiders those crops draw,
our wilder bounty. And there are woodsheds
and woodpiles, honeycombed with spider eggs
among the logs for year-round scavenging.
You couldn't ask for more nutritious grub!
Last August, I admit, a big black snake
discovered our nest tucked into a shed
and nearly ate us with our bite-sized brood.
This spring I've built a nest no snake can reach,
on top of the old couple's propane tank.
You've watched me, I know, fixing up this nook,
snug and well-roofed, and shaded from sunshine
that overheats the cubbyhole our cousin
house wrens just grabbed by the electric meter.
Let them have it! I say. This home's much better
to raise our nestlings in—and safely, too.
I'm sure the old homesteaders wouldn't mind;
frankly, I think they like our company.
So, sweetheart, shall we start a family?

Seasoned Tree-Huggers

There once was a cottager couple
who dwelled by a grove of mixed woods,
and they kept themselves sturdy and supple
with their gardens and hand-crafted goods.

They lived from their acres, in short,
and studied them closely each day
for new beauties and means of support:
four full seasons of good work and play.

Orphaned days—neither winter's nor spring's—
if well-lit gave a clear and far view
through bare woods of wild turkeys and things
fall and winter had left lying, too:

oak branches, dead elms, and red cedars—
sound timber for fences or heat—
to protect plants from deer, heavy feeders,
and burn well for a venison treat.

One such day—neither spring's nor quite winter's—
saw these cottagers gathering limbs
roughly pruned and some bristling with splinters.
The pair, grateful for what winter trims,

firmly hugged pieces carried to stacks
for new posts or stove wood, large and small,
to be sawn and well-split with an axe.
By day's end they had made a big haul

of found wood to be thriftily used.
For they knew with warm heart but cool head
to love trees, so were never confused
about honoring live ones or dead.

And the grove didn't grudge them their thrift
because deadwood removed made some space
for more trees, a renewable gift
with due credit to our human race.

Ashes to Ashes

I see the damage where woodpeckers strip
bark patches off—some deep wounds down to sap.
It's not a tree that any man would tap
(nor should he), but the avid peckers rip
into their work with whetted appetites.
They won't find all the larvae hatching there,
or eggs these come from. Worms the birds don't snare
survive as sapwood's deadly parasites,
boring to cut the life from its blood vessels.
Emerging adults, emerald-green, leave holes
my pencil can't fit in on stricken boles.
Soon many a winged beetle finds and nestles
in furrows of defenseless gray ash-bark,
unpecked as yet by any probing beak
which once more won't get all it's come to seek—
leaving more eggs to make their deadly mark.
So one by one the large and graceful trees
will die, left standing near countless stream banks.
Whatever fills their tall and crownless ranks
won't have bark diamonds Asian pests can seize,
or gemstone quality of strong heartwood,
I'm sure. The upshot here: a world made small
by careless hands of trade grows smaller all
the time, shrunk by this waste, this squandered good.

A Unique Hand-Me-Down

—in memory of Berthold Carl Huth—

Who'd ever use a spear to lay trees low?
I thought when my friend Paul grabbed a pike pole
his father made to guide them safely down.
Just over twelve feet long, hooked on the wall
of the garage, the shaft, harpoon-like, hung.
Tipped like that weapon with a metal point,
the barkless ash, perhaps three inches thick,
had for its lower end a wooden point.
Showing me how the tool was meant to work,
Paul, lunging, jabbed the shiny point at air
repeatedly, as when he'd drive the tip
firmly through bark and lodge it fast in sapwood.
The bottom tip, he said, should be "well heeled"
into the ground, making a solid prop
against the trunk the way it was to fall.
"That solves a problem geometrically,"
he went on, "since, whatever way it drops,
it can't fall back on you." Smiling, he added,
"I know you work alone in woods, like Dad,
and he'd be glad his pike pole kept you safe, too."
Another benefit became the norm
each time I used the hand-made tool: precision.
The first deadwood I dropped, in a small gap
between an oak and maple, proved the point.
That thick ash stub, a crownless thirty-footer,
my crosscut saw brought down without a hitch
midway between those trees—thanks to the pike pole.
More standing deadwood followed, each case quirky,
and then a daunting challenge, hard to handle:
a tall, dead ash festooned with poison ivy.
Not only leaves and hairy vines, but hundreds
of berries, small and white, made a false crown—
and that clung high above a path I walked
quite often, straight and densely canopied.

Oh, I considered ratcheting a heavy rope
to pull the tree down quickly when cut through.
But then that tonnage, topped with rampant ivy,
would trap the rope and ratchet underneath,
making more work—and no less dangerous—
than if I'd let the strangled tree's threat stand.
Besides, the same small space between two maples
a roped ash tumbled through could serve a pike pole—
assuming I had placed the pole precisely.
The ground, though, where its low tip had to stick
was full of rocks—it was a dry streambed—
and made a tricky place to press the point in.
Nevertheless I used some of those stones
to do just that, bracing the bottom better.
The top point, thrust already into sapwood,
was aimed right at what seemed a keyhole slot
between two trunks with crowns too high to snag.
This headroom, all the poison ash would need,
it slowly toppled through a short while later.
My sturdy, hand-me-down pike pole I reckon
has worked at least for sixty years to keep
its owners safe while felling problem trees,
but none, I'd swear, has dropped more beautifully.

A Widow-Maker

It's easy to lose track of just how long
a limb has dangled, loose, high overhead,
since you first noticed it. Unless I'm wrong,
you didn't see it fall when it was shed,
or note the broken joint it tumbled from.
Nor could you really know how well it lodged
in other upper limbs from where it's come
to gouge earth with a blow which can't be dodged.

You see, though, that the branch fell on a trail
you often wander. All you can do now,
aside from giving thanks it didn't hit
when you were there, is to uphold your vow
to watch the woods with more care—and not fail
to check deadwood, burning the best of it.

Parting Gifts

I see sun-catchers dropping, one by one;
their season-long work, feeding trees, is done.
Groves darkened by their green have finished turning
to yellows, golds, and reds, in sunshine burning.
I crave those colors lighting woods, unfallen;
yet when they drop at last, they will not smallen
their harvest realm, now warmly shimmering,
but make its glowing ground fit for next spring,
enriching home earth as a parting gesture.
Nothing is wasted, and as autumn's vesture
drifts slowly down, I pause and raise my cup
to economy kept whole and bottom-up.

A Message from Trees

Whose woods these are we know, and well.
He walks here most days for a spell
"To stir his stumps," he says, "and think
beyond a world of buy and sell."

He knows us for the ancient link
of deeper roots that breathe and drink
apart from greedy hand and mind
to keep earth whole. So in black ink

his flowering thought for us designed
preserved woods, land all green needs bind
into one deed for rooted heirs:
twin trusts forever, undersigned.

We stood and stand for faith he swears
to us and ours, and hope which dares
humans to honor their true shares
in wild growth kept to ease Earth's cares.

Dear Oom John

—for Joan Burroughs—

Dear Oom John,
It's been too long since we sat down together
like farmers, cussing and discussing weather—
as strange as ever, but crops hold their own.
Mine grow from good seeds, as they've always grown;
your celery swamp is just a memory, though,
and Slabsides is crisscrossed with trails, you know.
I go there now and then to see old timber—
still lovely, porch and all—and to keep limber
in thought, at least, climbing to Julian's Rock,
then rest a spell and of the times take stock.
I spot Slide Mountain in its Catskill range,
still standing tall beyond mere mortal change.
Yes, there the works of man dwindle and fade
as they cannot in towns made and remade
by wasteful trade whose watchword is: consume.
Households so crammed with things have little room
to think beyond life owned by purchased goods.
And workers rarely people fields and woods,
but flock to vast, machine-run neighborhoods
in cities; even farms are factories,
controlled by tractor fleets and crops they seize.
From their great roar to engines' hum and drone
in traffic, motors now have overthrown
the native music of our old homeland,
which fewer souls make time to understand.
Diminished warbler tunes enliven May,
while bobolinks lose nests to early hay.
The meadowlark's rare song grows rarer still,
and now at night I hear no whippoorwill.
Wild places still hang on, though under thumbs
of nobler human hands, maimed when war comes.
Beneath all this I sense man's ancient trust
in Mother Earth replaced by hardened lust

for power over her as untamed foe
first to subdue, then in small bits to know.
But she is no machine: organic ways
reject man's money-maddened, plastic phase.
Trees fail, as foreign sicknesses that stressed—
for heedless trade alone—our native best
blight elms, doom ashes, wilt the mighty oaks.
Yet all's not lost. Wild forest green that cloaks
our mountain slopes resurged, cut down no more
for charcoal; nor is any forest floor
littered with hemlocks, stripped for their tanbark.
Most hopeful is the widespread, growing mark
small landowners are making, giving back
good fields and woods for space wild creatures lack.
Some of us try, in short, to strike a balance
Earth needs to save its wild and human talents.
We look to you still to inspire our hearts
and minds through practical, time-tested arts.
Our outstretched hands, in joyful gratitude
like yours, received Earth's gifts; and in that mood
we pledge good use, as stewards so renewed.

Your Mindful New Paltz Neighbor

Aiming for Wholeness

The land had asked of them a certain height,
for what they came to was a garden orphaned.
So full possession of its promises
meant piecemeal labor on each plot in season.
Perennial crops came first, and they agreed
with gardeners who put in asparagus
and rhubarb, then debated all the rest.
Meanwhile they had a raspberry patch to rescue
from poison ivy's grasp and browsing deer.
They'd hardly thought of pulling ivy roots,
but that is what they did, with long, thick gloves
in winter—mindful of its toxic touch.
Protecting canes, they dug in cedar posts,
encircling them with wire fence six feet high.
Keeping wild mouths from raspberries makes plain
how long they labored and must labor still
to guard green beans or even yucca flowers:
a garden needs good warriors to grow well.
But fences cannot weed a patch of beets;
like every crop it needs strong, careful hands
to pull weeds fully, sparing tender roots
that swell all summer while they pick beet greens.
Newspaper mulch, just four sheets thick, they spread
between rows, stifling weeds and saving water:
good news or bad, their garden eats it up.
Leftover scraps get buried in the compost
with plant remains when harvest time is done.
This golden residue, new earth from rot,
is all they use to fertilize their ground.

It works, and costs them only brisk hand labor
to chop plant parts with corn knives, turn the pile
with spade or pitchfork, strain the rotting mix
through hardware cloth, and shovel "free" black gold
into a sturdy bag for ready use.
These dirt-plain facts direct their garden's care,
firm groundwork good earth asks of willing stewards.
Their twin goals—eating well while building soil—
they strive for, keeping whole with cherished land.
(At least they work to avoid the chronic curse
of humans' spoiling any place they settle.)
Yes, she and he won't challenge Nature's ways—
which made them and have stood the test of time.

A Poet's Preserve

What keeps a poet past his days?
Nothing, I'd say, but singing lines—
best if a living person raise
his voice, as that heart so inclines.
Yet what this poet worked by hand,
shaping his seasons as he learned
earthcraft stays, too: the very land
to which he, body and soul, long turned
for sustenance. Yes, that's no flight
of fancy, but an earthbound law
granting wild nature its sole right
to this same ground; so tooth and claw,
leaf and stem, bud and bloom remain.
These keep him, spirit and ashen bits,
in their rare space, past stress and strain,
and ringed by large old Shongum grits.
By law this right shall hold forever,
which a poet's passing cannot sever.

Set in Stone

I was a lucky dweller in daylight:
found rare fringed gentians next to dandelions,
smelled pink azaleas flowering out of sight,
and savored apples grown on tough wild scions.

I also witnessed winter's heartless night,
when wise men's words and deeds were scorned kinships;
and cursed machines' cruel waste—a man-made blight—
and felt war's loss in wild lives' quick eclipse.

Yet I for long knew no more fragrant wine
than sweet breath at requited love's warm lips.
For that lost life I'd sooner sing than pine
to keep its glow; but here my stone's old rite
lets flow, when dripping dew or ice or snow,
fresh tears of my own mingled joy and woe.

Defiant Life

Once dancing sperm and egg that paired in time,
I've grown to know an old, rare world of wonders.
Yet all, descended from primordial slime,
will end as dust—and be Earth's long-term funders.

Facing the certain mystery of demise
my living senses cannot penetrate,
I find no comfort in religions' lies
of next lives, but in knowing truth is great

and will survive all guesses at its forms,
which made and still make room—despite the pain
binding all beings and against the norms
of lifeless stars and darkness that remain
such vast, eternal powers to destroy—
for singing voices raised in bursts of joy.

A Garden Tip

A man with a song in his heart
can often come through or get by
crop failure or blight or a part
of beds of good blooms gone awry.

Yet often's not always, you say,
and gardening's gambling, we know.
So what is this gardener's way
to rescue a season brought low?

He answers, "Hold fast to the best
and, working with it, play along;
but as for the worst and the rest,
be sly and invent a new song."

A Cooperative Venture

My pole bean patch has friends and enemies.
A buzzing bumblebee is always free
to pollinate all blossoms it can seize;
long beans I get are worth its finder's fee.
Likewise, a mantis preying on old foes—
bean beetles—never wears its welcome out.
And when bean season's drawing to a close,
I watch orb weavers spin and hang about
round webs to wrap their victims in a snug
straitjacket, then drain them of insect blood.
Might this extend to fluids a stink bug
possesses, sometimes fouler than dog mud?
I wondered. When I caught one on a bean—
ready to eat a hole in tender flesh—
and dropped it in the orb, the spider'd seen
my gift, soon tightly bound in silken mesh,
and drank a full, deep draught—so long I left
to pick more beans, still large, green, and unharmed.
It's good to call a predator so deft
my friend, by nature stink-proof and well-armed.

Yuletide Greens

They're not what you are thinking of, I'll bet—
neat wreaths and sprigs purloined from needle-trees—
nor are they what I dreamed I'd find, and yet
this crop survived far more than one hard freeze
to grace a feast—fresh-picked from melting snow.
True, solar rays did help—through window panes
I took from worn-out frames and placed just so
they tilted south and shed ice-sharpened rains.
And I admit that garden patch has soil
well-worked for crops rotated twenty years,
rewarding its old tiller with less toil
than when hoes' hard rock music boxed his ears.
The secret, if it is one thing, I'm guessing
is kept by compost: seeds of plain Swiss chard
would not grow two-foot leaves without side-dressing
they loved—as well as fences standing guard,
of course, to keep unwelcome mouths away.
Yes, home-made compost it must be, and based
not just on garden clippings day by day,
but kitchen scraps, and laced with critters' waste.

Yankee Yucca

Unlikely dweller by a leaching field
far from its usual home in desert land,
the sword-leafed plant left in our care revealed
an unknown gardener's pointed sleight-of-hand.
So here this cactus cousin, made for heat,
thrives thirty winters later, no mean feat
though still within its unsubdued raw powers:
grown tall and full in eye-high magic wands
lined for a spell with spilled creamcups of flowers.
Deer relish petals, their wild salad course
shared by a human palate that responds
to home-grown flavor, not some store-bought source.
Deer even dared to browse green bayonets
through deep snow, aggravating winter's threats—
till I outfenced them, metal besting teeth.
But this plant needs no help and is no fluke:
its strong roots grasping rocky soil beneath
blades aiming at points north their sharp rebuke.

Hardscrabble Sweetness

So fernlike but no fern,
trail-neighbor of blueberries
for which my taste buds yearn,
how well that sweet scent carries!

Uphill one shrub group lurks
unglimpsed but smelled to tell
keen noses where it works
around the clock to sell
flowers only to itself
while, unseen, charming air,
like some spellbinding elf,
to feed roots in its care.

Lodged in dry, sandy places,
its acid earth sun-struck
year-round in many cases,
this native gets weird luck
by not being good to eat
yet near what is: wild berries
I'm always glad to meet
at bogs in pitch pine aeries.

Sweetfern keeps on, apart
but not begrudged its art
of fixing nitrogen
for breakfast, lunch, and dinner—
with thrift. Moreover, when
I stroke soft leaves, again

the aroma from the start
well names a tough old winner.

Rhapsody for *Spiraea Latifolia*

A country road meanders with a stream
where fishermen employ their famous flies.
My love and I walk there not to daydream
of trout in summer but to botanize.
By now we know most flowers' favored spots
near this Cat's Kill we've not yet seen a cat in—
for instance, soapwort or forget-me-nots—
but just for fun we're brushing up our Latin
to make odd common names more orderly.
So jewelweed we've learned to call *Impatiens*,
and red *Monarda*, not Oswego tea,
draws hummingbirds for needed deep libations.

Though *Solidago* holds massed goldenrods
in place (and keeps out trees), black *Rubus* fruits
grow sparse in shade, and yellowjacket squads
spoil more than any human eats or loots
for later baking in a luscious pie.
But that's no matter to fast-growing forest.
While granting woods their wild way, she and I
look past our loss—to foragers the sorest—
toward gaps which floods and gully-washers make,
freeing raw earth for *Rubus* to arise
with seedbank kin that next spring stirs awake.

Such blooming wealth will fill more than our eyes—
or bellies, by and by—and charm our noses
with plants not good to eat like meadowsweet
(*Spiraea*), milder-scented than most roses.
Though lacking *Rosa*'s thorns, it puts down feet
to stay in ditches or in bottomland:
for tiny clustered blooms long since outdid

Egyptian monuments' stone strength, and stand
their ground with flowers' perennial pyramid.

Gathered through the Grapevine

If you take country walks on old dirt lanes,
you see vines decorating wilder woods.
There's woodbine creeping with its tendril disks,
and Asian bittersweet plaguing more plants,
and home-grown poison ivy everywhere—
or so it seems just when you need to grip
a handy tree to slip past undergrowth.
Then there is grape, sometimes with vines so thick
you might think you could climb their trees with them.
"How did they get up there?" ask city people,
pointing at lofty tops of evergreens
or, just as often, crowns of rangy elms,
invading cedar spikes with cross-grained hardness.
The likely answer is the trees and vines
grew up together, rising heavenward
slowly, maybe beyond a man's strained vision,
in growth rings stretching old folks' memories.
One of those elms, scraping the sky for decades,
died awhile back but kept on standing there,
false-crowned with green grape leaves and fruit aplenty,
which birds and squirrels picked off, ripe or not,
then dropped their gifts of seeds throughout the woods.
Last fall a north wind snapped the elm's bare trunk,
and down the skeleton and vintage crashed.
Picking through wreckage for the soundest firewood—
letting tart clusters hang for wildling palates—
meant slicing thick rope every time I cut
a piece of elm, dead to its world but seasoned
for my use, if I needed heat that night.
(I didn't but my shed guards elm logs now.)

Needless to say, the grape was green inside
its shreddy bark the whole way down through roots—
perennial as any plant's can be.
Too much so, say some landscape *artistes*, branding
the fruitful native as invasive weed.
A weed is just a plant that's too successful,
that makes the best of what the world provides:
if only we were all so savvy, too,
say I. Oh, this old-timer should survive
my rough cuts and resprout to hitch a long,
slow ride up on a well-placed seedling tree;
I've seen it happen over and over again.
Wild grapes know how to grasp the earth and sky.

Most Invasive

This one grows everywhere, it seems:
on land, of course, but in such places
as mountains, swamps, near lava streams,
in deserts. There are more than traces
around both poles; large colonies
on favored coasts in warmer zones;
under sea level, if it please
the wanderlust bred in their bones.
The problem is, once swarms take over,
then everything is up for grabs;
whatever cannot run for cover
is doomed. Slashed forests form large scabs
on burning land, which may be dug
up further, tunneled in, or flooded.
Survivors—from a tiny slug
to bull moose—must avoid cold-blooded
or careless conquerors that claim
those spaces to the last square feet;
and poisons spread to kill or maim
the holdouts make conquest complete.
Someday these beasts that learned to fly—
a recent, clever adaptation—
may find the means they flourish by
undo their finite, Earthly station—
straining the bounds of truth and science
too far, forgetting basic stuff
dinosaurs learned the hard way: giants
felled by Earth's meaning of enough.

A Finder's Art:
The Right Stuff in a Natural Order
—for B.A.P.—

Finding ripe blackberries on near-bare canes,
she hunts beneath the few she nabbed for more,
hidden by leaves maybe, but found through stains
on sticky hands, and so she picks a score
while catbirds cry alarms. Unheard but seen,
stray canes in goldenrod lure her with jewels,
where at her feet black clusters flash their sheen.
She kneels long for sweet dewberries that fools
in blind haste partly trampled. She takes care
to pry the prostrate plants up with the tip
of her old shepherd's crook. In sun-drenched air
big berries gleam and somehow seem to drip
with scents her tongue and taste buds revel in.
She fills a heaping quart before she stands
and sees each dark-stained pantleg's knee and shin.
Yet she is hardly done; more bramble-lands
keep eyes and fingers busy, as her crook
lifts up large, hidden fruit on leafy stems.
Another quart fills as she probes this nook,
then adds some trailside pickings to those gems.
As meager as the wild crop first appeared,
its quirky fruitfulness confirmed the truth
of deeper riches, cropland many-tiered
that needs the senses of a patient sleuth.
Back home she ponders this while spreading out
the freshly rinsed black forms to dry on towels:
white paper holding essences no doubt
as meaningful as consonants and vowels
arranged for ready use at the right time.
Likewise, ripe berries frozen in their prime
keep choices for this seasoned cook sublime.

A Snake's Strange Story

The black snake, over four feet long,
was quite as thick as black snakes get,
and—though its writhing showed how strong
it was—well caught by one fine net

around our lone blueberry bush:
not meant to capture snakes, but keep
out beaks of any feather, push
back slyly at the hop and creep

of furry groundlings with sharp teeth.
Yet by nightfall it was the fate
of that black snake to wear a wreath
strangely designed by—ah! but wait

to hear just what, and how, and why.
At half-past noon one sultry day
in mid-July, my love's sharp eye
saw wriggling, only steps away

from our back door, of that large snake,
so tangled that, squirm as it might
(and did) for its own mortal sake,
escape was thwarted by its fight.

Pity for this trapped being raged
with fear in me, as searing sun
baked all below; so I assuaged
both crippling tortures then in one

way, watering the thirsty beast,
which swallowed trickles from my pail
with upturned, open mouth, at least.
More water poured on every scale

relieved the captive and me, too.
But other tasks took me away
till sundown streaked the sky's deep blue.
By then the snake in stillness lay—

its writhing spent—awaiting night.
I'd hoped that strength or cleverness
might free the reptile from its plight,
but it looked caught for good, unless

its human captors could release
it from their webbed, unnatural trap.
Though we were hardly snake police,
somehow we had to bridge that gap

if this poor being might yet survive—
and keep its natural control
of rodents dangerously alive.
Oh, then I searched my mind and soul

for how to free the beast—as caught
as chance that got it *and* me stuck
had shown, bound with need's moral Ought.
One answer loomed: to make my luck

with careful courage, dressed and gloved.
Protected thus, I grabbed the tail
and pulled—as one who truly loved
his homestead's tenants could not fail

to try—and wrenched the long snake free.
Released though wearing something queer
it coiled nearby, and I could see
a tattered wreath, its souvenir

of netting, ripped but clinging fast.
More help I dared not offer, hoping
instead that slithering would at last
undo the snake's unlucky roping.

Quite soon it did slink toward the forest
and darkness, home—and refuge, too.
Day dwindled, crickets sweetly chorused,
and trees' tall silhouettes regrew.

Twilight drew out this quiet glow
my love and I, with no regrets,
shared—glad our drama ended so—
as we began to mend the nets.

One Haymaker's Tale:
A Healthy Dose of Switchel

You'd hardly think a drink of cold well water
could do that till you've seen it for yourself.
But there I was in broiling mid-July,
stacking "square" bales of timothy six-high
on Warren's wagon, rolling through the field
behind the baler. Scott was on the ground,
hoisting to Don and me the wirebound bundles
as they dropped from its chute, each oblong cube
of grasses weighing maybe fifty pounds.
At least two wagonloads into the morning,
all three of us were shirtless, melting freely.
When Warren stopped the tractor to reload
the baler with more wire, we ran to shade
beneath an oak conveniently nearby.

Soon Verna, Warren's wife, drove her truck there
with jugs, jars, *and* a picnic basket lunch
(for later, she said, meanwhile smiling archly).
"Don't drink the water too fast, boys," she cautioned;
"you'll get a stomach ache. I know you're thirsty,
but take your time, and try some switchel, too."
"That's this brown stuff? I thought it was root beer,"
Don blurted, disappointment in his voice.
"It's easy on your stomach," Verna countered.
"You've never heard about haymaker's punch?"
We shook our heads and mumbled "No" together.
"It's mostly water mixed with my hives' honey,
molasses-thick dark syrup Warren gets
when boiling maple sap, good vinegar
from his old uncle Virgil's cider apples,
a half-teaspoon of powdered ginger root
I grow in my greenhouse and grind real fine—

and there's a gallon of fresh home-made switchel.
It's perfect for your hot job, bucking bales,
and you'll be glad you drank it if you're queasy.
I'll leave it here in shade with lunch and water;
I have to tow these wagons to the barn."

As soon as she jounced off, Don raised a jug
of water to his mouth, gulping so loudly
that Scott and I rolled eyes and shook our heads.
"At least that old gal brought this with her lecture,"
Don, smirking, said while passing Scott the jug
of cold well water, only half-full then.
"Now lunch for breakfast," Don continued, chuckling.
"The work here starts so early I missed mine."

As he chomped on a ham sandwich, I sipped
from Verna's switchel jar, finding the flavor
sweet-sour and hoping it might ease my stomach—
which I would never dare let on about.
Then Scotty took the switchel jar before
I was quite done with it, and swigged some fast.
But it was too late. That cold water downed
moments ago in gulps was coming up,
and I backed off to give him room to heave.
I thought I heard those same sounds presently
hard by the old oak's trunk where Don had sprawled—
but at that point was retching on all fours.
Wide-eyed I watched Verna's warning come true,
like some experiment in chemistry
or physics class you learned could never fail.
Too bad those strapping boys were learning that
the hard way; I was glad I didn't have to.

When Warren, who by then had fixed the baler,
called out to start again, I rushed right over
to tell him what had happened, ruefully.
"Those big, strong idiots!" he yelled, eyes blazing.
"And you," he growled, slit-eyed, "just had the switchel?"

"Yes, sir," I answered, quietly but uncowed.
"I know rain's coming, so I'll work real hard,"
I added, firmly, and he saw I meant it.

"Well, son, you are the only man left standing,"
he slowly said, turning to smile at me.
"Let's show those jerks how much a skinny kid
and one old guy can do before the rain!"
his large, deep voice rang out to all in earshot.
"With thanks to switchel," I said to myself.

A Realometer

"As clear as mud," a man of skeptic bent
might say of Walden Pond's thick sediment.
Its waters Thoreau called Earth's eye, because
it takes in real life, and can't skip the flaws.
Now the clear lens he knew is growing green
with algae: swimmers make it a latrine
as thousands empty bladders underwater.
Nor is there any trick or magic blotter
to erase atomic weapons' fallout, mired
beneath the eye, its poison unexpired.
Another toxin, deadly in its aim,
killed fish some thought unworthy to be game.
What poison's left fouls mud: just man's to blame.
Such inconvenient facts the pond's large eye,
forever open, cannot fail to spy
and feel in tender cells which never lie.
False skeptic eyes may blink real truths away
but can't remove what's deeply stuck in clay.

To Climate Skeptics

—for Dr. Ronald Pierce and in memory of Prof. Carroll Johnson—

One of the oldest, basic laws
of physics surely gives me pause
when I brood on our warming planet.
Because there is no way to ban it
from how the world exists and works,
and no deep mystery still lurks
to cloud one's grasp of what it means
alike for wage-slaves, kings, or queens,
its simple truth can't be ignored.
Consider: energy is stored
or live—potential or kinetic,
as physics teachers say. Prophetic,
in turn, of what all power lets loose
when it is tapped for any use:
heat, always heat. This is the law
our universe cannot redraw.
Now ponder myriad peacetime ways
(not counting figures for each weapon
blind statisticians miss or step on)
demanding energy these days
to feed, clothe, house, move, cool, and warm
our coddled species' swelling swarm.
Earth's temperature could rise quite high;
there are eight billion reasons why.

Devolving by Unnatural Selection

So much does not depend on red wheelbarrows
and never did: the whole of Genesis,
for instance, or a clutch of nestling sparrows.
But man-made things wild Earth will hardly miss,
or his false god of smooth convenience.
Whatever built our globe used sterner stuff,
forms many a harsh eon neither blunts
nor tames: old plants and germs, organic, tough.

Mankind may wish itself above this fray
and think its brainpower solely will suffice.
But who said reason stood behind the way
Earth's flowering was shaped by fire and ice,
or bets that smart machines could long hold sway
over wild matter? Care to roll the dice?

Note: The poem's first line is in response to "so much
depends/ upon/ a red wheel/ barrow," from "The Red Wheelbarrow,"
by William Carlos Williams.

Sound and Fury, to What End?

Now hear the shriek of motors driving air
that blows a trail of leaves across brown grass;
the whirring rumble of blades scraping bare
black pavement of its snow with each loud pass;
the slash of chainsaws on woods soft and hard—
no limb too large for chippers' guts to stow;
the roar of tractor-mowers on greensward,
not grazed by sheep or goats but grown for show!

Does it do you good to batter all ears
while saving strength to pamper swollen paunches?
What do you hope to gain by breathing, years
on end, foul fumes to spare long-fattened haunches?
Why estrange soft, idle hands from strong hand tools
by blasting power from Earth's bones, fossil fuels?

The Steadfast Poet

It matters not what current fashions do,
or why they chafe and scheme against the grain.
He sings unfazed the lines his soul finds true.

Impatient makers, lured by fast and new
line-spinning, toss out rhyme as too much strain.
It matters not what current fashions do.

The latest style abandons meter, too—
drumming a prosy rhythm, in the main.
He sings unfazed the lines his soul finds true.

Next goes the line, with thrusting sense it drew
and turned. What from this loss is there to gain?
It matters not what current fashions do.

Then figured speech and long-lived flowers it grew
are pruned. What from these losses can remain?
He sings unfazed the lines his soul finds true.

Yet one sure way around these snares is through—
chanting the firm belief, good work's refrain:
it matters not what current fashions do;
steadfast, sing well the lines your soul finds true.

A Double Crop

In spring few people rhapsodize
about a crop grown for its roots;
more plant their gardens with mind's-eyes
on store-bought seedling greens or fruits.
I'd keep imagination true
to what good seeds and soil can yield
all summer till this fall crop's due.
Long months before one beet root's peeled,
spice salads with first sprouts you thin
from crowded rows—almost like weeds—
but don't throw in the compost bin.
When each plant has root space it needs,
check red-veined leaves until they grow
as long as your own outstretched hand—
then pick some from each ample row.
These fresh greens palates understand
and savor in what's simply made:
a breakfast omelet, steamed treats
at lunch, at dinnertime sautéed,
in roasts or stews with any meats.
The ways to use greens don't end there,
of course, and—here's a happy fact—
these plants grow back more leaves to spare
as long as roots are left intact.
That harvest, starting when frost drapes
all but fall's sky, gives months to try
imagined dishes' varied shapes
beet greens may take on, by and by.
Make no mistake: I still eat beets
for their large roots, sweet to the core,
but leaves remind me that what meets
the eye holds in reserve still more
pleasures deep down I can't ignore.

Making the Most of It

Start with a sunny, well-drained plot of ground;
a small hilltop works fine.
Set posts to trace a line
five paces long, three paces wide, around
the arbor's shape, with overlong top beams
to frame its upper space,
crossbeams to hold in place
the vines that fill the arbor of your dreams.
To boost its yield and strengthen all its sides,
put in a middle row
for ranging vines to grow
so that the crop you can or freeze provides
in winter when your snowbound garden hides.
And snow's good fertilizer—
as every garden miser
knows, even those who author garden guides.
I'll take for granted that your soil's prepared
for seeding—though I do
oppose machines that spew
noxious exhaust. Food gardens can be cared
for with a hoe as tiller, then smoothed flat
by raking out the clumps
or levelling what humps
remain. Use both sides of your rake for that
two-step job; then you're ready for bean seeds.
Placed far enough apart,
what sprouts will from the start
have room as each root finds the earth it needs.
Pole beans will want good lattice-work to climb,
so guide vines, square by square,
aloft to open air
where there's good sunbathing for blossom-time.

Next, guard those vines from browsing deer with nets
each overlong top beam
(your clever building scheme)
hangs down to grass—all that a browser gets.
Then watch as sun and rain swell the green girth
of what you built from scratch
and sowed by hand, a patch
to learn how much a hill of beans is worth.

The Camera Never Lies?

—for David and Carrie Knudsen—

It's not science fiction,
this strip of bunchberries
(and whitely in bloom)
wedged in a constriction—
mere inches of room—
between boulder and slab.
The niche hardly varies
for a small plant to grab
more than crumbs of loose dirt,
but at least it's well-drained
so the rootlets aren't hurt—
meaning swamped when it's rained
cats and dogs the whole day.
Yet there's plenty of sun
for bunched flowers, then red fruit
when the blossoms are done—
and a photo, to boot,
of the stones and the greens
to suggest in its way
(and in jest, I must say)
that Ma Nature just means
here's a very hard roll
with a vegetable treat,
a sandwich some vole
may camp in and eat.

Serendipitous Meeting
—for Dr. Elizabeth Long—

September Swallowtail,
lone giant fluttering
from red to orange head
of zinnia blooms, you cling
for nectar till you're fed,
then past their post and rail
fly on to late coneflowers,
sunsplashed today for hours.
Perhaps you sense great shocks
beyond the equinox
tomorrow brings, but I'll
hope they hold off awhile,
if only for the sake
of trembling joy I see
and share as perfect wings
play at work noiselessly.
This flower for you I make,
not on your drinking spree,
pours out in all it sings
thanks for our give and take.

The Hardest Hue to Hold

Now come rare golden days, when hardwood trees
invite me for a stroll just as I please
to feel their light and breathe their atmosphere.
They've done this each fall since I settled here
to share the wealth of their wild neighborhood—
not that I'd dwell somewhere else if I could.
"Take in the beauty we have made for you,"
they whisper, rustling under deep sky-blue.
"All this endures, if you leave us in peace,
forever, and its great worth will increase."
I think hard on that "all," as I commune
with these truths long upheld by beings in tune
with earthbound ways and elemental means.
For more than threescore and ten times fall's scenes
have pressed their ripeness on my heart and mind,
unwearied by Earth's cycle, so designed
for permanence: regrowth atop decay.
My sole, long-held response is but to say,
as autumn makes its beautiful retreat
through old groves day by day: repeat, repeat.

A Snowbird Hangs On

—in memory of Hans Weber—

From a slate sky winged flecks of slate arrive—
just hours before frostbite eats through bean patches—
and claim white cedar roosts while they survive
the milder winter no far northland matches.
Weed seeds are uppermost in juncos' minds
as each flat pair of snowshoe-like feet scratches
out livings found on ground of many kinds—
not least where suet bits my garden catches
under a feeder. Still, there's always one
brave bird which flutter-hovers by the cage
dangling white fat well mixed with seedy parts.
Keen hunger helps him grip the bars' small gauge
his flock-mates tried to hold with all their hearts.
His feet grasp progress—and hang on till done.

After the Peak

If you have reached a summit you desired,
come down with care and savor the descent.
Absorb the rare, high prospects that inspired
your climb and what the hard steps up have meant.

But watch your footing on those places down,
where slips and falls may hurt inside much more
than missteps caught like pratfalls by a clown.
All the path back, in fact, might have in store

is not yet known—as luck which brought you here
to test the skills you learned and disciplined.
Courage you proved in conquering a fear
of heights, but thank those who braved this peak's wind
to blaze the trail through streams, up slopes, past boulders.
Half-jesting, say: I'm travelling on their shoulders.

About the Author

New Paltz poet Roger Roloff, author of six previous collections of poems, continues in *Windflowers* his long and fruitful exploration of Mother Earth firsthand. A homestead gardener with a song in his heart, he is loyal to traditional ways of making and turning the singing line: sonnets, rhymed couplets, villanelles, and blank verse, to name a few. Aided and inspired at home and afield by his wife, retired musicologist Barbara Petersen, he practices older, simpler means of living from the land while preserving its health. In essence the couple's own baker's dozen acres and fortunate surroundings in New York's Ulster County have given distinct and potent voices to these figurative blossoms, his windflowers.

About the Illustrator

In a career spanning three decades, Rachel Hunderfund (B.F.A., M.A.) has exhibited internationally, with works in private collections as well. She attended the Art Students' League in Manhattan, where she honed her figure-drawing skills. She received a merit scholarship from the Woodstock School of Art, where she studied with Hongnian Zhang and Lois Woolley. She also attended the Art Institute of Florence/Lorenzo de Medici, studying with Rose Shakinovsky and Claire Gavronsky, very influential in developing her style and technique. Also certified in yoga practice and instruction (C-IAYT, CYT), Rachel uses her creative skills in these disciplines, for they remain strong guides in her art and life.

CPSIA information can be obtained
at www.ICGtesting.com
Printed in the USA
BVHW06s2012051018
529422BV00013B/74/P

9 781605 714325